# A CENTURY *of*
# BEXLEY

Harvesting at Warren Farm, Bexleyheath, August 1903. According to a note on this picture by the photographer, A.H.T. Boswell, the lady's name was Gertrude. The buildings of Warren Farm can be made out in the distance.

# A CENTURY of
# BEXLEY

## MALCOLM BARR-HAMILTON

SUTTON PUBLISHING

First published in the United Kingdom in 1999 by Sutton Publishing Limited

This new paperback edition first published in 2007 by
Sutton Publishing, an imprint of NPI Media Group
Cirencester Road · Chalford · Stroud · Gloucestershire · GL6 8PE

British Library Cataloguing in Publication Data
A catalogue record for this book is available from the British Library.

ISBN 978-0-7509-4930-9

*Front endpaper*: Houses being built by Aylings on the Martens Grove Estate, Barnehurst, 1934. This
photograph, looking north up Watling Street, was taken from the top of Crayford Gas Works. The arch
leading into the estate is advertising houses from 13s 9d weekly.
*Back endpaper*: Patrons of the Royal Oak, Bexley Road, Northumberland Heath, outside the pub, *c.* 1900.
Dating from the 1860s, it was entirely rebuilt in 1930.
*Half title page*: Mr W. Hurst, gentlemen's hairdresser, in front of his 'Gentleman's Hair Cutting Salon' at nos
210–12 The Broadway, Bexleyheath, near Banks Lane, *c.* 1920. Hurst was established there in about 1909,
taking over from a hairdresser called B. Flory, and remained until the 1930s.
*Title page*: Penton and Dean, gentlemen's outfitters, Erith High Street, 1920s. In a directory for 1903 Penton
and Dean had premises at 1 High Street described as 'Boot Stores'; by 1905 they were at these premises,
17 (formerly 8b) High Street and described as Kent Clothing Stores. In the late 1930s they moved to
20 Pier Road.

Typeset in Photina.
Typesetting and origination by
Sutton Publishing.
Printed and bound in England.

# Contents

Crofton Avenue, on New Ideal Homesteads' Albany Park Estate, Sidcup, *c.* 1933. The houses are 'LB' type which cost £425 when they were new. They give the appearance of being large semi-detached houses but are in fact in terraces of four. The pylon and telegraph hardly make up for the absence of trees. Except for milk, the delivery of food supplies to houses had all but died out by 1990; however, since then a number of local supermarkets offer such a facility, and increasingly goods can be ordered via the Internet.

# Britain: A Century
# of Change

Children gathered around an early wireless set in the 1920s. The speed
and forms of communication were to change dramatically as the century
advanced. (*Barnaby's Picture Library*)

The delirious rejoicing at the news of the Relief of Mafeking, during the Boer War in May 1900, is a colourful historical moment. But, in retrospect, the introduction that year of the first motor bus was rather more important, signalling another major adjustment to town life. In the previous 60 years railway stations, post-and-telegraph offices, police and fire stations, gas works and gasometers, new livestock markets and covered markets, schools, churches, football grounds, hospitals and asylums, water pumping stations and sewerage plants had totally altered the urban scene, as the country's population tripled and over 70 per cent were born in or moved to the towns.

When Queen Victoria died in 1901, she was measured for her coffin by her grandson Kaiser Wilhelm, the London prostitutes put on black mourning and the blinds came down in the villas and terraces spreading out from the old town centres. These centres were reachable by train and tram, by the new bicycles and still newer motor cars, connected by the new telephone, and lit by gas or even electricity. The shops may have been full of British-made cotton and woollen clothing but the grocers and butchers were selling cheap Danish bacon, Argentinian beef, Australasian mutton, tinned or dried fish and fruit from Canada, California and South Africa. Most of these goods were carried in British-built-and-crewed ships, burning Welsh steam coal.

As the first decade moved on, the Open Spaces Act meant more parks, bowling greens and cricket pitches. The first state pensions came in, together with higher taxation and death duties. These were raised mostly to pay for the new Dreadnought battleships needed to maintain naval superiority over Germany, and deter them from war. But the deterrent did not work. The First World War transformed the place of women, as they took over many men's jobs. Its other legacies were the war memorials which joined the statues of Victorian worthies in main squares round the land. After 1918 death duties bit even harder and a quarter of England changed hands in a few years.

Women working as porters on the Great Western Railway, Paddington, c. 1917. (*W.L. Kenning/ Adrian Vaughan Collection*)

The multiple shop – the chain store – appeared in the high street: Sainsburys, Maypole, Lipton's, Home & Colonial, the Fifty Shilling Tailor, Burton, Boots, W.H. Smith. The shopper was spoilt for choice, attracted by the brash fascias and advertising hoardings for national brands like Bovril, Pears Soap, and Ovaltine. Many new buildings began to be seen, such as garages, motor showrooms, picture palaces (cinemas), 'palais de dance', and the bow-windowed, pebble-dashed, tile-hung, half-timbered houses that were built as ribbon-development along the roads and new bypasses or on the new estates nudging the green belts.

During the 1920s cars became more reliable and sophisticated as well as commonplace, with developments like the electric self-starter making them easier for women to drive. Who wanted to turn a crank handle in the new short skirt? This was, indeed, the electric age as much as the motor era. Trolley buses, electric trams and trains extended mass transport and electric light replaced gas in the street and the home, which itself was groomed by the vacuum cleaner.

A major jolt to the march onward and upward was administered by the Great Depression of the early 1930s. The older British industries – textiles, shipbuilding, iron, steel, coal – were already under pressure from foreign competition when this worldwide slump arrived, cutting exports by half in two years and producing 3 million unemployed (and still rising) by 1932. Luckily there were new diversions to alleviate the misery. The 'talkies' arrived in the cinemas; more and more radios and gramophones were to be found in people's homes; there were new women's magazines, with fashion, cookery tips and problem pages; football pools; the flying feats of women pilots like Amy Johnson; the Loch Ness Monster; cheap chocolate and the drama of Edward VIII's abdication.

Father and child cycling past Buckingham Palace on VE Day, 8 May 1945. (*Hulton Getty Picture Collection*)

Things were looking up again by 1936 and unemployment was down to 2 million. New light industry was booming in the Home Counties as factories struggled to keep up with the demand for radios, radiograms, cars and electronic goods including the first television sets. The threat from Hitler's Germany meant rearmament, particularly of the airforce, which stimulated aircraft and aero engine firms. If you were lucky and lived in the south, there was good money to be earned. A semi-detached house cost £450, a Morris Cowley £150. People may have smoked like chimneys but life expectancy, since 1918, was up by 15 years while the birth rate had almost halved. The fifty-four hour week was down to forty-eight hours and there were 9 million radio licences by 1939.

In some ways it is the little memories that seem to linger longest from the Second World War: the kerbs painted white to show up in the

A family gathered around their television set in the 1950s. (*Hulton Getty Picture Collection*)

blackout, the rattle of ack-ack shrapnel on roof tiles, sparrows killed by bomb blast, painting your legs brown and then adding a black seam down the back to simulate stockings. The biggest damage, apart from London, was in the south-west (Plymouth, Bristol) and the Midlands (Coventry, Birmingham). Postwar reconstruction was rooted in the Beveridge Report which set out the expectations for the Welfare State. This, together with the nationalisation of the Bank of England, coal, gas, electricity and the railways, formed the programme of the Labour government in 1945. At this time the USA was calling in its debts and Britain was beggared by the war, yet still administering its Empire.

Times were hard in the late 1940s, with rationing even more stringent than during the war. Yet this was, as has been said, 'an innocent and well-behaved era'. The first let-up came in 1951 with the Festival of Britain and then there was another fillip in 1953 from the Coronation, which incidentally gave a huge boost to the spread of TV. By 1954 leisure motoring had been resumed but the Comet – Britain's best hope for taking on the American aviation industry – suffered a series of mysterious crashes. The Suez debacle of 1956 was followed by an acceleration in the withdrawal from Empire, which had begun in 1947 with the Independence of India. Consumerism was truly born with the advent of commercial TV and most homes soon boasted washing machines, fridges, electric irons and fires.

The *Lady Chatterley* obscenity trial in 1960 was something of a straw in the wind for what was to follow in that decade. A collective loss of inhibition seemed to sweep the land, as stately home owners opened up, the Beatles and the Rolling Stones transformed popular music, and retailing, cinema and the theatre were revolutionised. Designers, hairdressers, photographers and models moved into places vacated by an Establishment put to flight by the new breed of satirists spawned by *Beyond the Fringe* and *Private Eye*.

In the 1970s Britain seems to have suffered a prolonged hangover after the excesses of the previous decade. Ulster, inflation and union troubles were not made up for by entry into the EEC, North Sea Oil, Women's Lib or, indeed, Punk Rock. Mrs Thatcher applied the corrective in the 1980s, as the country moved more and more from its old manufacturing base over to providing services, consulting, advertising, and expertise in the 'invisible' market of high finance or in IT. Britain entertained the world with *Cats*, *Phantom of the Opera*, *Four Weddings and a Funeral*, *The Full Monty*, *Mr Bean* and the *Teletubbies*.

The post-1945 townscape has seen changes to match those in the worlds of work, entertainment and politics. In 1956 the Clean Air Act served notice on smogs and pea-souper fogs, smuts and blackened buildings, forcing people to stop burning coal and go over to smokeless sources of heat and energy. In the same decade some of the best urban building took place in the 'new towns' like Basildon, Crawley, Stevenage and Harlow. Elsewhere open warfare was declared on slums and what was labelled inadequate, cramped, back-to-back, two-up, two-down, housing. The new 'machine for living in' was a flat in a high-rise block. The architects and planners who promoted these were in league with the traffic engineers, determined to keep the motor car moving whatever the price in multi-storey car parks, meters, traffic wardens and ring roads.

Carnaby Street in the 1960s. (*Barnaby's Picture Collection*)

11

The Millennium Dome at Greenwich, 1999. (*Michael Durnan/Barnaby's Picture Collection*)

The old pollutant, coal smoke, was replaced by petrol and diesel exhaust, and traffic noise. Even in the back garden it was hard to find peace as motor mowers, then leaf blowers and strimmers made themselves heard, and the neighbours let you share their choice of music from their powerful new amplifiers, whether you wanted to or not. Fast food was no longer only a pork pie in a pub or fish-and-chips. There were Indian curry houses, Chinese take-aways and American-style hamburgers, while the drinker could get away from beer in a wine bar. Under the impact of television the big Gaumonts and Odeons closed or were rebuilt as multi-screen cinemas, while the palais de dance gave way to discos and clubs.

From the late 1960s the introduction of listed buildings and conservation areas, together with the growth of preservation societies, put a brake on 'comprehensive redevelopment'. Now the new risk at the end of the 1990s is that town centres may die, as shoppers are attracted to the edge-of-town supermarkets surrounded by parking space, where much more than food and groceries can be bought. The ease of the one-stop shop represents the latest challenge to the good health of our towns. But with care, ingenuity and a determination to keep control of our environment, this challenge can be met.

# Bexley: An Introduction

Any elderly person alive in the Bexley area in 1900 would have considered that they had lived through a time of considerable change locally. For in the nineteenth century there had been more drastic change than for several hundred years previously. In the north Erith had grown from a small riverside village into a major industrial town and a new suburban district called Belvedere had been developed. In the central area Bexleyheath had developed during the course of the century from a virtually uninhabited heath to a populous town; and in the south the dormitory town of Sidcup had sprung up. As an integral part of this development, three railway lines now cut across the district. It must have been hard to imagine that the twentieth century could bring with it even more drastic change. Yet it did, imperceptibly at first, and then, in the 1930s, at a breathtakingly rapid rate, as nearly the whole of the district was given over to one huge suburban sprawl.

In spite of the significant developments that had taken place in the nineteenth century, the administrative framework and the boundaries of the several administrative areas were virtually the same as they had been for centuries before and which to a large degree survived until the creation of the London Borough of Bexley in 1965. Though the Local Government Act of 1894 brought with it the new terms of urban and rural district councils they were applied to the areas of ancient parishes. The boundaries of Bexley Urban District Council were those of the ancient parish of St Mary's, Bexley, including Lamorbey, Bexleyheath and much of Welling; indeed, these boundaries can be identified as those of the Manor of Bexley as described in an Anglo-Saxon charter of AD 814. Similarly, the Erith Urban District coincided with the ancient parish of St John's, Erith. Crayford, not having a large enough population to be classed as an urban district, formed part of the Dartford Rural District but had its own Parish Council (it gained the status of an Urban District in 1920). The Parish of East Wickham, curiously, was also in the Dartford Rural District, though 'landlocked' from the rest of it. (This anomaly was rectified when it was transferred to the Bexley Urban District in 1902.) In the south Footscray and

North Cray had their own parish councils but formed part of the Bromley Rural District Council.

In 1901 the size of the population of the Bexley area was 52,500. Development was relatively slow in the early years of the century with the census of 1911 showing an increase of about 13,000. New developments were close to the existing major centres, with streets of Edwardian houses in Erith, Belvedere, Bexleyheath and Sidcup. New public facilities such as public halls, new churches and pubs, and the first cinemas were developed. An important innovation was the electric tramway operated by the Bexley and Erith Urban District Councils. This form of cheap and reliable public transport led to the development of working-class housing in Welling, Bexleyheath and Northumberland Heath for workers in the Thameside industrial districts of Erith and Woolwich. The First World War had a significant impact on the district because of the location of arms manufactories at Erith and Crayford, and in nearby Woolwich; the large influx of munitions workers was located chiefly in Welling and at Crayford where, as a result, the size of the population trebled.

The junction of Upton and Lion Roads, Bexleyheath *c.* 1905. In spite of the rapid growth of Bexleyheath in the nineteenth century, the pattern of farms and country lanes on its outskirts was largely undisturbed. Upton was a web of country lanes, and the hamlet had no definable centre as such. Though now largely built up, the ancient pattern of lanes survives.

14

After the First World War, a new phase of development began as many of the old landed estates, no longer economically viable, were broken up into plots suitable for building and the Housing Acts of 1923 and 1924 stimulated council housing schemes. Yet, for all this, by 1930 the area was still predominantly rural, with market gardening prevalent. But this was to change and change very quickly, for by the outbreak of the Second World War much of the area had altered beyond all recognition as fields gave way to housing estates at a phenomenal rate. The causes of this development are a combination of factors including electrification of the railways, road building, the failure of agriculture and most importantly the availability of government housing subsidies. Whole new districts came into being such as Bostall, Barnehurst and Falconwood and the old communities spread so that Erith merged into Bexleyheath, and Welling into Sidcup. This growth was not just destructive to agriculture; many fine old houses were swept away too such as Blendon Hall in Bexley and Marten's Grove in Crayford. Happily some were brought into public ownership and survived, such as Hall Place, Danson and Sidcup Place.

There were some significant changes in local government in the 1930s also. In 1934 Sidcup Urban District was merged with the parishes of North Cray, St Paul's Cray, Mottingham and Chislehurst

Crayford Way, Crayford, 1920s. This is part of the Barnes Cray Estate built by Vickers for munitions workers between 1915 and 1916. Over six hundred properties were built in a variety of styles, each containing at least three bedrooms and a sunny living room, and were supplied with hot and cold water. Their architect was Gordon Allen who specialised in vernacular style housing developments.

Urban District to form the new Urban District of Chislehurst and Sidcup. In 1937 Bexley was successful in its bid to gain borough status, the most apparent benefit of which was the right to have a mayor. Erith followed suit in 1938.

The Second World War had a devastating effect on the Bexley area, which suffered because of its proximity to London and its industrial targets in the north. Altogether 508 civilians were killed, 1,990 sufficiently injured to be detained in hospital and 3,463 suffered minor injuries. 2,120 properties were totally destroyed, 3,792 severely damaged, and 92,597 slightly damaged. (Note these figures include the whole of the Chislehurst and Sidcup district.)

After the war suburban growth continued but not with the same dynamism that characterised the 1930s. While some significant amounts of open space had been preserved from the march of bricks and mortar before the war, such as the 600 acre Danson Park and over 100 acres at Hall Place, the Green Belt Act of 1938 saved more thanks to its 'Green Belt Girdle' for London. Footscray Meadows

Hurst Road, Bexley, looking north, 1938. The houses shown were built by New Ideal Homesteads earlier in the decade. New Ideal Homesteads built more houses in the borough than any other single development, with huge estates in Sidcup, Bexley, Welling, Barnehurst and elsewhere. The trees are part of Hurst Farm which was not developed until after the Second World War. Hurst Place, however, survived as a community centre.

survived in this way. They were purchased by the Kent County Council in 1946. In the 1950s the central and southern parts of the district had become very much a dormitory suburb characterised by the male of the family working in London and commuting by train; while in the north industry continued to flourish. Neither had agriculture been altogether extinguished. While administratively still a part of the county of Kent, the economic and geographic reality was that the area had greater links with London than with its historical county town of Maidstone. It was perhaps the north of the district that particularly felt some gratitude to the London County Council, who had safeguarded the wonderful open spaces of Abbey Woods and neighbouring Bostall Heath. Following the 1963 Act of Parliament, in 1965 the London Borough of Bexley was created out of the Boroughs of Erith and Bexley, the Urban District of Crayford, and that part of the Urban District of Chislehurst and Sidcup north of the A20. The choice of the name 'Bexley' was unfortunate, for it gave the impression, particularly among the proud peoples of Erith and Crayford, that they had been

In spite of the massive amount of development that has taken place throughout the twentieth century, some aspects of the London Borough of Bexley have changed surprisingly little. This view is taken from near Parsonage Lane, North Cray, as it approaches Joydens Wood, looking towards Bexleyheath in 1999. On the left is Gattons Plantation and on the right is Joydens Wood.

'taken over' (perhaps with some justification), feelings which still linger nearly 35 years later. However, the choice of a name could not have been easy and using an existing name would inevitably upset some. The best that could be suggested in terms of a 'neutral' name was the 'London Borough of Kentgate'! Perhaps the use of a very minor place name such as Ruxley would have been the best option. To this day space in the letter columns of the local papers are devoted to the discussion of whether Bexley is in Kent or London.

However, even before the emergence of the new local authority, two important developments were afoot, both in the north of the borough. One was Erith Borough Council's plans to rebuild the town centre (which has been an unmitigated disaster) and the other was the London County Council's plan for building a new town on marshland straddling the Erith/Woolwich border. This, of course, is what we now know as Thamesmead, a name (uncontroversial as far as I am aware) selected in a *Kentish Times* competition by a reader in Barnehurst.

In spite of the extensiveness of pre-war development, scope has been found for further initiatives; mainly in terms of infill on odd bits of land and on redundant industrial sites and railway sidings. Since the 1970s there has been much redevelopment, usually involving the demolition of large Victorian houses and their replacement with blocks of flats and sheltered accommodation.

Since the 1970s there has been a trend for Bexleyheath to become the 'centre' of the borough, both administratively with its civic offices and commercially with the establishment of the Broadway Shopping Centre as the borough's main retail area. The future of Bexleyheath as a major shopping centre is in doubt as the twentieth century draws to a close – in the spring of 1999 the new Bluewater Regional Shopping Centre opened virtually on its doorstep.

A significant development over the last 35 years of the century has been the steady growth of ethnic minority populations in the Borough which are starting to provide a rich cultural diversity. The 1991 census showed the 'non-white' population to be nearby 6 per cent of the total, the largest of the many different ethnic groups being Indian (2.4 per cent). These figures will be significantly higher in the census of 2001.

At the close of the twentieth century the Bexley area remains very much part of suburbia, and a popular place in which to live. It is hard to imagine it changing as drastically in the twenty-first century as it has in the twentieth, but who knows?

# The Start of the Century

The clock tower, Bexleyheath, under construction, 1911. This edifice, built by public subscription to commemorate the coronation of King George V, was opened in 1912. It remains today as one of the last tangible links in Bexleyheath's town centre with its early past. In recent years it has been enhanced firstly, in 1990, with the replacement of the bust of the king (the original of which had disintegrated decades earlier), secondly, in 1997, with the addition of a bust of William Morris (Bexleyheath's most famous resident) and thirdly, in 1998, when the clock and its chimes were brought back into action for the first time since 1914! The Pincott Memorial drinking fountain to the left commemorates the Revd H.W. Pincott, first Vicar of Bexleyheath, who died in 1878 aged only forty-three after tirelessly devoting himself to the parish. Sadly it has been moved to a much less prominent position outside Christchurch.

Mount Road, looking west from Upton Road in about 1905. The development of the Upton district of Bexleyheath from the middle of the nineteenth century was slow and piecemeal. The northern side of Mount Road can be seen as largely developed with a variety of detached, semi-detached and terraced houses. The south side did not get built on until the 1930s. In the middle distance the Royal Oak public house, otherwise known as the 'Polly Cleanstairs', can be seen. On the left hand side are some old cottages known at this time as Hankey's Cottages, after John Alers Hankey, the owner of the Mount Estate. The Mount itself was a sizeable mid-nineteenth-century house just to the south of Mount Road (see page 33).

Passengers leaving Erith railway station, *c.* 1910. Erith's beautiful station building of 1849 survives to this day and was restored in 1994. It was thought that the arrival of the railway might enhance Erith's aspiration to be a desirable resort town but in fact, conversely, it hastened the industrialisation of the area as witnessed by the factory of Fraser and Chalmers to be seen behind the group of young ladies. These respectable-looking middle-class ladies are no doubt returning to their villa-style houses in the sought after Lesney Park district of the town.

Erith Yacht Club, early 1900s. Yachting had been popular on the Thames since the seventeenth century. The first yacht club in Erith was founded in 1872 as the Corinthian Yacht Club. Its clubhouse was opened in June 1879, and in 1893 it became the Royal Corinthian Yacht Club. In its heyday it had over 300 yachts on its list, but the increase in commercial traffic on the river obliged the club to leave Erith in 1898. In 1900 the Erith Yacht Club was formed using the Corinthian's old premises seen in this picture. The steps on the left lead up from Corinthian Manorway.

Belvedere recreation ground, showing Albert Road on the right and the bandstand behind the children, early 1900s. This recreation ground is a remnant of the original Lessness Heath (which was the original name for this district before 'Belvedere' was adopted). An act of parliament of 1818 secured the enclosure of Erith's common land. Nine acres of Lessness Heath were supposed to remain as common land but this had been significantly reduced by the time it was made into this popular recreation ground.

A house in Elm Road, S
c. 1900. Sidcup possess
great many large detac
semi-detached houses
the incoming upper-m
classes who moved to t
town as it developed fo
the opening of the Dar
Loop Line in 1866. Elm
was developed on what
been a footpath. The fa
of this rustic-style hou
posing in an informal
for the Sidcup photogra
Alfred Dewey.

Manor Farm barn, Ruxley, c. 1900. This building was the old parish church of St Botolph's, Ruxley, dating from
twelfth century, though excavations carried out in the 1960s revealed the footings of an even older building. The p
of Ruxley had dwindled by the mid-sixteenth century to under double figures and in 1557 the building was dec
and the parish united with that of St James, North Cray. It was subsequently used as a barn. After many years of c
the state of the building, restoration work was carried out in 1993–4, largely funded by English Heritage.

Bexleyheath Post Office, 1910. It was built between 1903 and 1905. Notice that Bexleyheath is still spelt as two words whereas, supposedly, it had officially been changed to one word towards the end of the nineteenth century. The building is still in use as the town's post office although there have been threats to close it. The attractive pair of houses to the right survive too, though converted to shops. The right hand one, which was partially rebuilt following war damage, was where the Revd Pincott once lodged.

Avenue Road, Erith c. 1916. This avenue of elm trees was originally the approach to Erith Manor House, built by William Wheatley in 1769. Though the house was demolished in 1858, the elms remained until they were felled because of Dutch elm disease in the early 1970s.

Hatherley Road, Sidcup, *c.* 1904. Hatherley Road had been laid out by the early 1870s as part of the great transformation of Sidcup from little more than a hamlet in 1860, to a populous town by 1900. These extraordinary looking houses were built for upper-middle class families who were moving from the more densely-populated inner-London suburbs. While most of these houses have disappeared in recent years to make way for small blocks of flats, some of these richly ornamented buildings have survived.

Pincott Fields, Bexleyheath, *c.* 1900. These fields, part of Warren Farm, took their name from the Revd H.W. Pincott, the first vicar of Bexleyheath. The view is looking east and is the site of what later became Latham Road. The strawberry pickers (some of whom may well be Londoners) are taking a break from their labours. The district was noted as a fruit-growing area and this was further enhanced following the opening of the Bexleyheath Railway in 1895, which made the London market more accessible.

The opening of the Baptist Mission in North End, 1919. This rather primitive looking building in Arthur Street was operated by Queens Street Baptist Church in Erith to cater for the rather isolated community of North End which was in the parish of Crayford. The Revd J.E. Martin, who was minister at Queens Street Baptist Church for 55 years from 1875 to 1930, is the man with the white beard in the front row, a little to the left of the new mission building.

Physical instruction lesson at Sidcup Hill School, *c.* 1918. This school was built in 1907 by the Kent County Council which in 1903 became the education authority for the whole of the present Bexley London Borough area, except Erith, which remained an education authority in its own right. The school is typical of the KCC village schools of this era, and indeed still perpetuates something of a village school atmosphere to this day. It survived a closure attempt in 1992–1993.

'Slades Green' Canary Club members outside the post office, Slade Green Road, *c.* 1910. Though Slade Green is now the accepted term for this district, controversy continues as to which is the more correct. The origin of the name is probably from the Saxon 'slade' meaning a low lying spot, as little of the land thereabouts is more than ten feet above sea level. The district was developing in the early twentieth century following the building of the South Eastern Railway Maintenance Depot in 1899, and it is quite likely that some of this male-dominated group of bird lovers were railway workers. The shop is now a hairdressers.

Bexleyheath Gala parade passing along The Broadway, *c.* 1900. Bexleyheath's annual gala was an important day in the town's calendar. It was held in Danson Park courtesy of Mrs Bean, the owner, and was preceded by a procession from the town centre. The mid-Victorian shops survived until 1999 when they were demolished for a new shopping development. The trees to the right of the shops are in the grounds of detached and a pair of semi detached villas, set back from the road. These later became the site of W.T. Richards' Garage (see p. 75).

Entries in the most beautiful baby competition, Bexleyheath Gala, Danson Park, 1912.

The Revd Wicksteed in the Vicarage Garden, Bexley, c. 1903. Wicksteed was the Vicar of St Mary's, Bexley for thirty years from 1893 to 1923. The occasion is possibly the annual church bazaar. The vicarage, in Vicarage Road, near its junction with the North Cray Road, was built in the late nineteenth century. It is now a home for the elderly called St Mary's Home.

The Revd and Mrs F.W. Porter, *c.* 1912. The Revd Porter became co-pastor of Trinity Baptist Church in the Broadway, Bexleyheath in 1912; he served as pastor for an astonishing forty-seven years. Throughout this time he was supported by his wife.

Maypole dancing, Sidcup Vicarage, July 1904. St John's in Sidcup possessed a large vicarage, set in extensive grounds, an ideal spot for such a display shown here. It was demolished in 1937 to make way for Invicta Parade. Maypole dancing is considered to have its origins not so much in folklore as Victorian invention.

rayford High Street, looking north om Crayford Bridge, *c.* 1902. On the ft is part of the Bear and Ragged Staff ublic house. In the late-seventeenth entury there was a pub on this site lled the Half Moon but from about 728 it got its present name. For a ort time in the mid-1990s, owing public outcry, it was renamed the range Kipper but has now reverted its traditional name. On the right Ockwell's chemist's shop which ccupied this advantageous site from e 1890s to the 1930s. In front of is a police box which was destroyed a runaway steam lorry in 1907. rtually the whole of the right-hand de of the High Street was demolished part of a widening scheme in 1938 t a number of old buildings on the t-hand side survive.

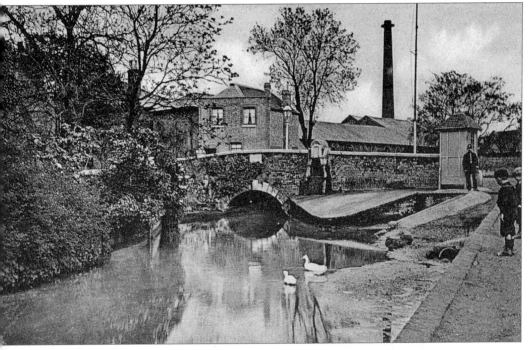

rayford Bridge, *c.* 1907. This view shows the bridge built in 1755 by the New Cross Turnpike Trust which was responsible that time for this important road from London to Dover. It replaced an earlier bridge, but as the name of the town viously implies, the River Cray was originally crossed here by means of a ford. The bridge was widened in 1920 and is side rebuilt in 1938. The drinking fountain seen on the bridge now stands in nearby Cray Gardens. It commemorates evenson Arthur Blackwood who died in 1880. He was an evangelist preacher who lived at Crayford Manor House.

Rectory Lane, Footscray, *c.* 1910. This view is taken from the junction of Rectory Lane (or Church Road, as it was then called) with Footscray High Street and shows the premises of G. Groombridge, cycle maker, prior to moving to Sidcup Hill. The fine three-storey Georgian houses known as Belgrave Place still remain, but the two-storey ones, including Groombridge's shop, have been demolished.

Salisbury Road, Bexley, *c.* 1910. This development of relatively modest and mainly semi-detached houses built in a field on the north of the railway line bounded by the High Street and Hurst Road, dates from the early 1890s. The houses are characterised by unusual diagonally-arranged decorative timberwork. The street remains substantially the same today though the trees and fences have generally made way for car-parking spaces.

Bexley Mill and Bridge House, Bexley, 1910. There has probably been a mill on this site since early times. Domesda Book tells us that Bexley had three mills, and it is likely that one of them was on this site. The building shown here dated from around 1779. At the time of the photograph it was in the occupation of Cannon and Gaze Ltd, steam corn millers. It was destroyed by fire in 1966 and replaced by a virtual replica which opened as the Old Mill pub and restaurant in 1972. The eighteenth-century Bridge House to the right was demolished shortly after the Second World War.

...senden Road, Belvedere, c. 1900.
...is was part of the Eardley family's
...lvedere Estate, which was developed
...r housing in the 1850s following the
...ening of the North Kent Railway
...1849. These substantial detached
...operties with extensive gardens were
...nong the grandest in this desirable
...sidential area. Like a number of
...eet names in Belvedere, Essenden
...ad takes its name from a place in
...rtfordshire where the Eardly family
...d other estates.

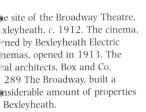

Cross Street decked out for Erith Town
Regatta, 1909. Erith has long used
the River Thames for recreational
purposes, and the first yacht club in
the town was founded in 1872 as the
Corinthian Yacht Club. Erith Town
Regatta was founded in 1886, and
as can be seen from this photograph
must have generated a great deal of
excitement in the town. Cross Street
was demolished in the mid-1960s.

...e site of the Broadway Theatre,
...xleyheath, c. 1912. The cinema,
...ned by Bexleyheath Electric
...nemas, opened in 1913. The
...al architects, Box and Co.
...289 The Broadway, built a
...nsiderable amount of properties
...Bexleyheath.

The opening of the Bedon Stream pent stock and floodgate scheme, Belvedere by the local MP James Rowland in 1909. This was a scheme sponsored by the Erith Urban District Council as an Unemployment Relief Scheme. The gentlemen standing on the newly-erected dam wall near Vinson's Farm are, from left to right, an unidentified reporter from the *Erith Times*, Mr Frewel (the editor), W. Ling JP (Chairman of the Erith Distress Committee), James Rowland (MP for the Dartford Parliamentary Division), and T.H. Bell (Secretary of the Erith Distress Committee).

An Erith Council tram in Bexley Road, Northumberland Heath, *c.* 1907. Following the introduction of electricity into the Erith Urban District in January 1903, the Urban District Tramways began operation in 1905. This was part of the main line which ran from Abbey Wood. At Northumberland Heath an end-on junction was achieved with the Bexley Council Tramways which had opened in 1903. The pub to the left of the tram is the Duke of Northumberland, the first purpose-built pub in Northumberland Heath, dating from the mid-1860s.

Welling High Street, looking east from near the junction with Danson Lane, 1900. This photograph indicates a fair amount of rebuilding in late Victorian times when a number of smart new shops replaced quaint old cottages. A couple of the latter can be detected in the distance. The Rose and Crown, the sign of which can be seen, had been rebuilt after a fire in the 1870s. The land immediately around the High Street was still very rural at this date.

A Rolls-Royce at the Mount, 1910. The Mount was a large mid-Victorian house on the southern slopes of Bexleyheath. Much of its former grounds now comprise Bexleyheath golf course. There were many such houses in the Bexley district at this time which gave employment opportunities for the villages and hamlets associated with them. The gentleman about to get into the impressive car is probably Sir Charles Tupper, the former Prime Minister of Canada who resided at the Mount at this time.

Blendon Hall, *c.* 1900. The impressive country house was rebuilt for Lady Mary Scott in 1763. There must have been an important house here in medieval times when Henry de Bladingdon and such like are recorded. It stood in grounds of 88 acres on the southern side of Blendon Road. It was demolished in 1934 and the estate developed for high class housing by D.C. Bowyer and Co.

A winter scene at Halfway Street, Sidcup, looking east towards Holy Trinity Church, *c.* 1910. Halfway Street was an ancient self-contained hamlet until the opening of the Dartford Loop Line in 1866 from when it gradually merged with Sidcup. The buildings, centre right, are Church Cottages.

'Gallant Belgian Wounded & Red Cross Staff, Crayford 26/10/14.' By October 1914 a growing number of Belgian refugees were being housed locally. The *Bexleyheath Observer* reported on 16 October that six had arrived in Bexley in the previous week, three ladies staying with Mr E.B. Kelsey, butcher, of Bexley High Street and three gentleman staying with Mr V.G.M. Colt of Mount Mascal, North Cray. In East Wickham and Welling a home for refugees was set up at Cromwell House. This photograph was probably taken at Springfield, a large house on the Crayford/Bexleyheath borders where the Crayford Committee for providing hospitality to Belgian refugees had established a home.

The Drill Hall, Erith, 1915. This was occupied by men of the Royal Defence Corps who were guarding the munitions works at Erith. The Drill Hall was on the south side of Fraser Road and was later replaced by one in Park Crescent.

The Rodney YMCA hut, Crayford, *c.* 1917. This building, which stood by the River Cray close to Vickers Works, was erected the memory of Lt William Rodney of the Rifle Brigade and the Royal Flying Corps, who was killed in action in France in 191 The hut was opened by his mother, Lady Rodney, on 7 June 1915 in the presence of a large and distinguished audience, f the use of HM munition workers. Its objects were to promote the social, physical and spiritual welfare of the workers.

The Queen's Hospital, Sidcup, *c.* 1918. The house, called Frognal, dates mainly from the seventeenth century and w the home of the Townshend family. In 1915 it was empty and in 1917 a collection of prefabricated buildings was s up in the grounds as a military hospital and called the Queen's Hospital. Frognal itself was converted to provide nursi accommodation, administration and a mess for convalescing officers. The hospital became internationally famous for advanc in facial plastic surgery under the leadership of Sir Harold Gillies. In 1930 the hospital was renamed Queen Mary's Hospital.

e staff of Bexley Council Tramways. *c.* 1916. The staff are seen in front of the tram shed in Bexleyheath, on the south le of the Broadway. As a result of the war female conductresses had been introduced. A similar picture dated 1920 shows at by then the staff was once again male dominated.

Vickers Vimy in
e assembly hangar,
rayford, 1918. Aircraft
anufacture had begun
t Crayford in 1912. The
imy was perhaps the
est known of the aircraft
anufactured here, as it
as in one such machine
hat Alcock and Brown
ade the first flight
cross the Atlantic in
919.

The Victory tram car, August 1919. This Bexley Council Tramways car ha[s] been extravagantly decorated with the flags of the victorious allied nations and other trappings. Something of a controversy surrounded it as the decision to decorate it was not taken at a properly constituted meeting of the council, and employees were not allowed to work on the decorations in council time.

The reopening of the Princesses Theatre, Crayford, 1919. The theatre, built for the benefit of the munitions workers, was originally opened in July 1916 by HRH Princess Christian and HRH Princess Victoria (hence the name) but was very badly damaged by a fire in December of that year. The Duke of York, later George VI, who re-opened it can be seen coming out of the car in the centre. In the background some of the newly-built houses forming part of the Barnes Cray Estate for munitions workers are visible. The theatre, which subsequently became the Ritz Cinema, was demolished in 1957 for a parade of shops, but the foundation stone still remains. The ornamental lamp-posts have been removed to outside a garage in Bourne Road.

The 'Peace Treat' in what was later known as Franks Park, 11 July 1919. This huge gathering of children was not the only event in Belvedere to mar[k] the signing of the Treaty of Versailles. There was also a Belvedere Peace Carnival in the grounds of the Royal Alfred Institution (Belvedere House) about a month later.

# Between the Wars

The staff of the Town Clerk's Department, Bexley Charter Day, 30 September 1937, when Bexley Urban District became a borough. The Town Clerk, Mr W. Woodward, is in the centre and Mr H. Griffiths, the Deputy Town Clerk, is to the left of him. Bill Brooker, now a mainstay of the Bexley Historical Society, is on the extreme left of the third row back. The staff are posed outside the front entrance to the council offices in the Broadway. The Charter Ceremony took place in Danson Park.

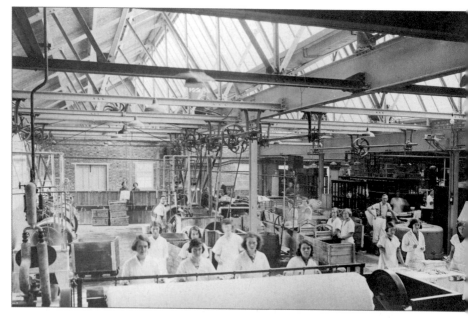

The washroom at the Bexleyheath and District Laundry, 1920s. This business was established at the junct
of Pincott Road (now Norwich Place) in about 1908. It survived until the 1960s.

8. ERITH. FRASER ROAD.

Fraser Road, Erith. *c.* 1920. Factory workers returning home. The factory of Fraser and Chalmers, to the ri
of the picture, from which Fraser Road got its name, was built in 1891 on a site which had previously be
used as a recreation ground. It manufactured steam plant, milling machinery, and general engineering.

Class 1 at Slade Green Primary School, June 1922. This school had been founded in 1868 to serve the remote and isolated rural community of Slade Green in the parish of Crayford. It was originally a National School (Church of England) but was handed over to local authority control in 1938.

Pelham Farm, Bexleyheath, early 1920s. Part of the farm was developed by New Ideal Homesteads in 1932, and part was given over as a site for Pelham Primary School.

Bourne Place (behind the tree) and Humphrey's Farm, Bexley from Rochester Way, September 1934. The sig
refers to car park construction in connection with the Robin Hood. The name eventually chosen for this lar
road house was the Black Prince, apparently at the suggestion of Lady Limerick of Hall Place. Any connectio
between the Black Prince and Hall Place is, of course, quite unfounded.

Blackfen, 1920. At this time Blackfen was still little more than a hamlet centred at the junction of Blackfe
Road with Westwood Lane and Days Lane, with some development in Days Lane. This view is taken from th
Blendon Road at its junction with Penhill Road, which can be seen to the right of the fence.

Penhill Park shopping centre site, early 1930s. A parade of shops was soon to be built on this site for New Ideal Homesteads' Penhill Park Estate. The newly-built Sherwood Park Avenue is to the left of the sign, at its junction with Penhill and Blendon Roads. Such local shopping parades have had mixed fortunes in the latter part of the twentieth century, as competition from large superstores has forced many small shops to close.

A new parade of shops on the south side of the Broadway, Bexleyheath, 1932. Neo-Georgian was the favoured style for parades of shops in town centres in the 1920s and 1930s, with mock-Tudor generally, but not universally, being reserved for more localised parades. This parade was demolished in the early 1980s to make way for the Broadway Shopping Centre.

The junction of Bar
Road with Erith Roa
looking towards
Bexleyheath, *c.* 193
Ellingham Ltd, a Da
based firm, purchas
67 acres of woodlar
farmland from the l
family in 1926 for
on which it was pla
build 578 houses. B
started in the same
it was not until 193
all the houses were
The estate agents, A
Kent and Co., contir
operate in the Broac
until the late 1980s

Hillingdon Road, Barnehurst, *c.* 1933. These newly-built houses were part of Ellingham's Barnehurst Estate. All th
were built of red brick with tiled roofs to a common design but with an option on internal layout. All had space t
garage.

Kelvin Road, Welling, looking south from its junction with Bellegrove Road, 1934. This development was built on the small country seat of Bellegrove Park, sold for building in 1929. The houses, many of which were built by George Perfect, were some of the most prestigious in Welling.

Wessness Park, Bostall, awaiting demolition in 1933. This large mid-nineteenth century Italianate villa, the estate of which fronted Woolwich Road, was developed as an estate mainly of bungalows by Messrs Thoburn. All that survived was a fine line of trees in Woolwich Road and a small portion which became West Heath Recreation Ground.

Little Danson, 193
attractive house on
south side of Welli
Street was built in
early nineteenth ce
for Hugh Johnston
Johnston family of
The Little Danson I
was developed in t
1930s but the hou
survived until just
the Second World V
when its site was u
the Embassy Ballrc
p. 74).

George and Henry Cowell's, tobacconists and confectioners, 1930s. This shop was no. 3 Midfield Parade, Barnehur
Cowell is seen with his sister Babs. It was Babs who was responsible for dressing the windows which took her a whole
shop has now become the Barnehurst One Stop Convenience Store.

John Burton outside his shop, 'The Fruitery', no. 143 Blendon Road, Bexley, c. 1936. This was one of a new parade of shops built in 1935 opposite the Three Blackbirds public house. Mr Burton and his family came from West Ham where he was finding it difficult to get regular work as a boiler maker/welder. He ran the shop until 1959; it is now a pizza restaurant.

Long Lane, Bexleyheath, c. 1937. This shows the transformation of Long Lane from a country lane to a suburban road nearing completion. The picture is taken looking north from the railway bridge over the Bexleyheath line. In the centre, to the left of the steamroller, is Sheldon's Farmhouse, soon to be demolished, and to the right of the steamroller, the Yacht public house covered in scaffolding, nearing completion. To the left an orchard awaits its fate.

One of F.L. Williams' fleet of cars, 1920s. Williams' shop was at no. 37 High Street, Bexley, and the garage fo his hire cars was in these former stables in what is now called Oxford Mews behind shops on the south side o the High Street. The premises are still connected to the motor trade, now called Autocare. This view is lookir west towards Salisbury Road.

Stevens Ltd, transport department, *c.* 1926. Stevens, a Woolwich-based building firm, were one of th largest developers in the district particularly in the northern parts of Welling. In the early 1930s they wei completing a hundred houses a week. The company had its own sand and gravel pits and also, for a time, i own brick pits. The transport department, seen here, was at Little Danson in Welling High Street, the site no occupied by Embassy Court.

Whittle's 'the sign people' sign painting workshop, Bexleyheath, 1930s. This well-known local firm was situated at 176 The Broadway. The signs being worked on are all of a local nature. Reffells' Brewery was in Bexley village, and the St Audrey Estate was one built by Absalom's on the north side of Long Lane, near the railway bridge. Whittle's claimed to be 'experts in modern publicity'.

Weston's Stores' staff outing, 1937. It seems probable that friends and relatives are accompanying the staff of Weston's 'Cut Price Grocery' on their annual trip, no doubt to the seaside. The shop was at no. 111 High Street, Erith.

The Sidcup bypass showing recently-installed traffic lights, 1938. This road had been opened in 1924, one of the such roads to be built in the country. Its construction was a significant, though not crucial, factor in the rapid deve of the district in the 1930s. This view is of Frognal Corner, looking west to Hoblands Wood which the road has bis the 1980s Sidcup bypass was considerably upgraded and this junction replaced with an elevated roundabout.

St Martin's Church, Barnehurst, nearing completio 1936. Many churches locally were built or rebuilt 1920s and 1930s for different denominations and new parishes were carved out of older ones for the new communities which had sprung up so rapidly Martin's was built on a large scale out of red brick very much of its era. The interior is imposing with brick arcades. A sanctuary was added in 1972.

50

The interior of Church Garage, Sidcup, 1934. The rapid growth of Sidcup in the second half of the nineteenth century saw many churches of various denominations established. This corrugated-iron building in Hatherley Road was opened as a Baptist church in 1890, providing sittings for two hundred people. The church moved to its present site in Main Road in 1922. Though now demolished, the site is still in use in the motor trade as the Whitehouse Van Centre.

Mayplace School, Barnehurst, 1930s. The site for this school, part of the Oakwood Estate, was purchased by Education Committee in 1932 and the school was opened by Lord Northbourne in December 1933. The scho but destroyed by fire during an air raid in September 1940; it was rebuilt in 1946. This postcard was published Cowell's of Midfield Parade (see p. 46).

Erith High Street, early 1930s. In any view of Erith Causeway there are always men (usually elderly) leaning on watching the river. Behind the men is the Yacht Tavern showing signs of having recently been refronted. It was d in 1938 as part of an 'improvement' scheme and the licence was transferred to the newly-built Yacht public hou. Lane, Bexleyheath (see p. 47). To the left is Erith Police Station, built for the river police in 1908. In the dista unmistakable silhouette of the Cross Keys, rebuilt in 1892.

rith Hospital, 1920s. The first Erith Hospital was established in 1871 in Sun Cottages, Crayford Road, and only offered
ve-beds. In 1875 it moved to a large villa with twelve beds. This attractive Cape Dutch style building with its elaborate
entral Dutch gable was opened by the Prince of Wales (later King Edward VIII) in 1924.

he first trolleybus
utside the new depot in
rith Road, Bexleyheath,
935. Trams disappeared
arlier in this part of the
netropolis compared to
ther parts where they
urvived until the 1950s.
he trolleybuses were a
reat success and passenger
gures rose. They in turn,
hough, gave way to motor
uses in 1959.

A meeting of the Chis
and Sidcup Urban Dis
Council, 1934. Follow
Kent Review Order of
the new local authori
Chislehurst and Sidcu
District Council was e
in 1934. This combin
only the former urban
of Chislehurst and Sic
also the parishes of M
North Cray and Pauls
One benefit of this wa
for the first time the v
the town of Sidcup w
the boundaries of one
authority, whereas pre
significant parts of th
area had been in Chis
The new authority's c
at Sidcup Place, The (
Sidcup, a country hor
from the eighteenth c

Sidcup Public Library, 1935. The first public library opened in Sidcup as late as 1930, in six rented rooms over s
corner of Sidcup High Street and Hatherley Road. Demand was such that in 1932 the library moved to these i
premises of the eighteenth-century Hadlow House in Hadlow Road. Unlike the urban districts of Bexley and Erith
district of Chislehurst and Sidcup was not at this time a library authority, and library services were provided I
County Council.

The path by the Danson Road end of the lake, Danson Park in the 1930s. In 1924 the Bexley Urban District Council purchased what was left of the Danson Estate, including the mansion and 200 acres around it. It was opened as a public park by Princess Mary in 1925. While Hall Place remained a private residence, the council developed Danson Park as the district's prime leisure facility.

Martens Grove swimming pool, 1933. In 1932 Crayford Urban District Council had purchased an area of 22 acres of woodland and parkland, part of the Martens Grove Estate. It included this ornamental lake which was converted into a swimming pool for just £150. The charge for admission was 3d for adults and 1d for children. It was replaced by a new pool which opened in 1939 and survived with intermittent closures until the mid-1980s when competition from heated indoor pools and a lack of commitment from the London Borough of Bexley resulted in its demolition.

Bexley Cricket Club, 1925. Bexley Cricket Club can trace its origins to the beginning of the nineteenth century, and may well have been formed as early as the eighteenth century. This team picture includes the club's most famous player, Arthur Wellard, third from the left, second row from the back. His parents kept the Black Horse in Albert Road. After a highly successful period with Bexley he joined Somerset CCC in 1927, qualifying to play for them in 1929, and for the next twenty years, apart from a break for the Second World War, he was one of the leading bowlers in the country, regularly taking over a hundred wickets a season. But he is perhaps best remembered for his powerful batting and in the course of his first-class career he hit some 500 sixes accounting for a quarter of all the runs he made.

Fancy dress parade, Bexley, 1938. This
apparently taken in the yard of Reffells'
Bourne Road, Bexley is of an event whi
part of Bexley Cricket Week. The popula
weeks were first held in 1903 and 1904
did not become a regular annual feature
1922. They regularly included a carniv
fancy dress parade through the village.
Waistell, the head of Reffells' Brewery, v
Chairman of the club from 1926 to 19
costumes display great imagination; qu
the girl fourth from the left in the front
supposed to represent, I have no idea!

The opening of the Regal Cinema, 3 September 1934. The square red-brick façade is typical of its architect, Rober
who designed a number of Regals. The Regal was in the 'super' cinema class with a 2,044-seat auditorium. It was
Sidney Bacon's Pictures Ltd.

# The Second World War
# and Postwar Period

King George VI at Bexley, August 1940. The King inspected various Air
Raid Precaution and Home Guard units in north-west Kent.

Canberra Road, Bostall, 1940. This house was demolished by a direct hit from one of several bombs dropped on 7 September, the first big day raid of the Blitz.

Elmhurst Auxiliary Fire Station, Bedonwell Road, Belvedere, 1940. Elmhurst was a large old house set back from the road. This picture of the AFS personnel and their equipment is presumably taken in front of the former stables. Elmhurst subsequently suffered a direct hit, killing one fireman and injuring six others. It was subsequently demolished and replaced first by temporary prefabs and then a council estate.

Learning how to use a stirrup pump, August 1940. The members of the Crayford fire party seem to be enjoying this lecture.

Blackfen youngsters helping with the salvage campaign, c. 1940. In the first month of Bexley's salvage scheme in March 1940, about 15 tons of salvage was collected and sold. This rose to 164 tons in March 1942.

An incident in Abbotts Walk,
Bostall, 15 October 1940.
A daylight attack resulted in this
crater, the full width of the road
outside nos 71 and 73. A baker's
van was sucked into the crater by
the counterblast but was able to be
driven away once pushed out.

Bexley Warship Week, 19
Mayor and other local dig
are assembled for a thank
service at the Regal Cinem
Bexleyheath. A staggering
£415,702 had been raise
the week, over half the cc
HMS *Lance*. The Mayor at
and addressed no less tha
one meetings during the
days and 'two charming 
the Warship Queen and h
attendant, were present a
thirty functions.

Crayford's Aid to Russia campaign, *c.* 1942. It seems today to be very strange to think of a picture of Stalin an
and sickle emblems being paraded around Crayford, but of course the entry of the Soviet Union into the war had 
vital factor in the Allies' effort. The people of Crayford certainly appear to have entered into the spirit of the event
authentic-looking costumes. The vehicle which had been loaned by Keevil's, the builders of Dartford, is seen outsid
Crayford Way.

The staff of the Plaza Cinema, Blackfen, Christmas 1944. The good people of Blackfen are having their morale lifted by seeing the film *Greenwich Village* starring Carmen Miranda, Don Ameche and William Bendix. Prophetically, the patrons are being wished a 'victorious new year'.

Longlands Road, Sidcup, 1945. Freda Skinner (née Greenway) and her brother Raymond are seen in a bomb-damaged Longlands Road. Their family home (no. 68) is behind them and on the left behind the fence is a war-time allotment.

A VE Day party, Royal Oak Road, Bexleyheath, 1945. Considerable enterprise and ingenuity is demonstrated by the provision of the food, decorations and costumes in hard times.

Bexley Dancing School, *c.* 1945, performing by the topiary at Hall Place, Bexley. Proceeds from this display these self-confident young ladies went to the Sunshine Home for Blind Babies. Over fifty years later there a still a great many aspiring ballerinas in Bexley, my two daughters included.

Development of the Springfield Estate, 1945. Building development had generally come to a halt during the war. It never again reached the same frenetic pace of the 1930s. Springfield, a small mid-nineteenth century mansion on the Bexleyheath/Barnehurst borders, can be seen in the foreground awaiting demolition.

Midhurst Hill, Bexleyheath, looking south, May 1947. This part of the former Pincott fields, was one of the last parts of Bexleyheath to be developed. Houses were soon to be built on this site, although the area on the left, part of The Warren, was left as open space.

A wedding party, June 1946. The wedding of Mr D. Mercer and Miss P. Flowers was at St Augustine's, Belvedere and this picture was taken in the garden of a house in Gilbert Road, Belvedere. The continuance of rationing after the war made this wedding a relatively simple affair. The bride was unable to obtain a formal white wedding dress and bridesmaid Joan Wood (on the extreme left) made her own. The reception was a simple home affair and the couple had their honeymoon in Ramsgate.

The Mayor's Ball, Erith, 1947. This event held on August Bank Holiday was the culmination of the weekend of the Erith Show and Sports. The venue is the Northumberland Heath School Hall. Music for these events was usually supplied either by the Royal Artillery Band or the Bert Fuller Band. A highlight of the evening was a beauty contest with the winner chosen by the crew of the visiting frigate HMS *Lennox* adopted by Erith during the War.

# The Fifties

The Odeon, Upper Wickham Lane, Welling, 1951. The Odeons were perhaps the best known chain of cinemas in the 1930s and were run by Oscar Deutsch. This was the first Odeon in the district, and was designed by the famous architect, George Coles. It opened in 1934. Ten years after this photograph was taken its function switched to a bingo hall.

Bourne Road, Bexley, 1951. This view is taken from the junction of Bourne Road with the High Street looking north. While some elements of the picture remain the same today, there have been some significant changes, the absence of traffic then being the most obvious. On the extreme left is Aldridge's fish and chip shop, an important village institution. The white building, centre left, was Bradbourne House, demolished in the late 1950s to make way for a parade of shops. In the centre is the entrance to Reffells' Brewery which closed in 1956 following its acquisition by Courage. To the right of the brewery sign is a terrace of four mid-nineteenth century houses which had been demolished by the end of the decade. To the right of these, with the van outside, is the former Baptist Chapel built in 1846.

Bexley Council Offices, Broadway, Bexleyheath, 1951. Oak House, as it was originally known, was built about 1817, making it one of the earliest buildings on the recently enclosed Heath. In the latter part of the nineteenth century it was a private school. It was purchased by the Bexley Urban District Council in 1903 for about £3,000, and was converted into council offices with a council chamber and a tramshed constructed in the grounds. It continued in this use, finally as the home of the Finance Directorate of the London Borough of Bexley until its demolition in 1978.

Crayford Urban District Council housing scheme no. 17, 1951. Crayford Council was a very active provider of council dwellings, undertaking 45 schemes between 1923 and 1960. These 'Easiform' semi-detached houses are at the junction of Birling and Chipstead Roads, Northend.

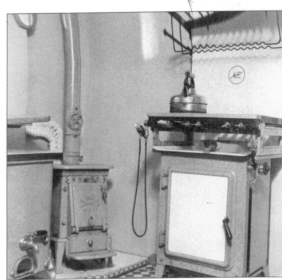

The kitchen of 144 Birling Road, 1951. Crayford Urban District Council provide the homes on this estate with the very latest in domestic appliances. There were over 170 dwellings provided on this estate.

East Wickham hutments, Lodge Hill, 1952. These huts had been put up quickly during the First World War, as temporary measure, to house the huge influx of munitions workers at Woolwich. They survived until the 1960

Erith Show and Sports, 1950. You could cut the tension with a knife in the very serious business of judgir the Caged Birds Society competition.

Beauty parade, 1951. Miss Valerie Council has just been chosen as 'Miss Festival of Bexley'. Many such events were held locally to tie in with the Festival of Britain. The ball had taken place at the Lord Kitchener public house in Wrotham Road, Welling.

Staff of the Chislehurst and Sidcup Urban District Council Treasurer's Department, 1950s. The latest in office machinery is complemented by the latest in fashion in this office at Sidcup Place.

The Embassy Ballrooms, Welling, 1951. This institution is remembered with affection by many Bexl
residents, though it was rather short-lived. It was built on the site of a large house called Little Danson (s
p. 46), part of the Danson Estate, in 1939, and demolished in the 1960s. The site is now occupied by t
Embassy Court shopping precinct.

Thanet Road, Bexley, in course of construction, March 1956. This view is taken from the Parkhill Road en
looking east. About seventy houses resulted from this development on backland behind the High Street. Tod
it tends to be used as a 'rat run' by motorists attempting to avoid the usual congestion in Bexley Village.

Richards' garage, 76 The Broadway, Bexleyheath, 1950s. Filling up with petrol was a much more pleasant experience than it is today, with two members of staff to assist you. W.T. Richards moved here in the 1930s. The garage later became the Lex Motor Co.

The interior of Hides department store, Bexleyheath, 1951. Hides started in 1851 when Henry and George Hide purchased the business of Collier's Emporium at 85 The Broadway. It gradually expanded and in 1936 was rebuilt as a modern department store. To the universal dismay of the local population Hides was destroyed to make way for the Broadway Shopping Centre in the 1980s. Try buying a needle and thread there!

The Broadway cinema, Bexleyheath, 1958. This cinema had been built in 1913 (see p. 31) and remodelled to give it this distinctive art deco appearance in 1929. By the end of the 1950s television was just beginning to prove the downfall of many cinemas. The Broadway was turned into a supermarket, trading under various names including Tesco and lastly Kwiksave. In 1998 it was converted into a public house, and in line with the fashion of the 1990s for exotic sounding pub names it is now known as the Rat and Parrot.

A display of televisions in Whomes' electrical shop, Bexleyheath, 1959. The Whomes family music business had been an important part of Bexleyheath since the nineteenth century when Mr Edward Whomes was organist at Christ Church. The business, by which time it was mainly dealing in electrical equipment, moved into the new Broadway Shopping Centre in 1983 but went out of business at the end of the decade faced by increasing competition from the multiples.

The opening of Hall Place Gardens, Bexley, 3 June 1952. Although the then Bexley Urban District Council had purchased Hall Place and grounds in 1935, the Countess of Limerick remained as tenant until her death in 1943. The gardens were opened by the popular Princess Marina, Duchess of Kent, seen here with the Mayor of Bexley and other dignitaries. They are seated in front of the west front of the older part of the building dating from about 1540. The beautiful gardens continue to be one of the borough's most popular attractions.

A young-looking Edward Heath (second from the left) handing in his nomination papers for the gen election of 1950. Heath had been chosen as the Conservative Party candidate for the Bexley Constitue in 1947. The other candidates are, from left to right, Charles Job (Communist), Ashley Bramall (Labour) Mary Hart (Liberal). Ted Heath polled 25,854 votes and had a majority over Labour of just 133 votes.

General Election leaflet, Margaret Roberts, 1951. Better known by her later married name of Thatcher, Margaret Roberts was unsuccessful in contesting the Dartford constituency which at that time included Erith and Crayford. She was beaten by Norman Dodds the Labour Party candidate by a majority of over 12,000. During the campaign she could be heard at, among other places, Crayford Town Hall and Erith Electricity Showrooms. The returning office reported that the contestants had 'fought th election in the best British spirit and withou personalities'. Meanwhile in the neighbouri constituency of Bexley, Mr Edward Heath w re-elected with a majority of 1,639. It was at this time that she met her husband, Den who was a director of the family paint and chemical firm, the Atlas Preservative Compa in Erith.

The Erith and Belvedere Football Club First team, 1958. The club began the 1958/59 season (in the Corinthian League) with a new manager, Charlie Revell (on the extreme right) who had made 224 appearances for Charlton Athletic at left half and scored 100 goals. Nevertheless Erith and Belvedere finished in a disappointing tenth place (out of fourteen). The top scorer in the season with 25 goals was Paul Sheckles (in the centre of the front row).

The Thames floods, 1953. Water pours through a breach of the bank near Callenders Jetty at the second tide at 2.30 p.m. on 1 February. On 31 January a storm surge driven by hurricane-force north-westerly winds smashed east coast sea defences and caused extensive damage to 1,000 miles of coastline. Across the Thames on Canvey Island 58 people were killed. Amazingly the death toll in Kent was only one, a nightwatchman at a factory in Crabtree Manorway, Belvedere.

Flooding in Station Road, Belvedere, 1953. The prominent building, centre left, is the Belvoir Tavern prior rebuilding in the 1960s.

Her Majesty the Queen meeting flood victims at St Augustine's Church Hall, Belvedere, 1953, some of who are finding the camera something of a distraction.

Crowds assembled in Riverside Gardens, Erith, awaiting the Royal Yacht *Britannia* with Her Majesty the Queen aboard, 1954. Despite a cold, biting wind many of these people waited hours for the happy moment when they could cheer and wave their flags.

Danson Park Lake, landing
stage and motor boat, 1951.
The launch, *Miss Lingrad*, was
home built in Bexley. Danson
Mansion can be seen in the
distance, and to the right the
old boathouse, later destroyed
by fire.

Old Age Pensioners' Coronation party, Crayford Town Hall, 4 June 1953. This celebration was rather unusual in that the food was prepared by 'housewives' who were all prospective members of the Civil Defence Corps (Welfare Section), along with enrolled Civil Defence volunteers and members of the Womens Voluntary Services, under emergency conditions. Army-type Soyer boilers were set up out of doors to cook the potatoes and boil water for tea and washing up. The meal consisted of ham, salad and creamed potatoes with fruit salad and ice cream and cakes, biscuits and tea to follow. Few of the pensioners appear to be enjoying the meal; perhaps the sing-song and concert that followed made them more cheery.

Rochester Way from Lodge Lane, looking east, 1951. The A2 – as it is generally known by those who speed along it – shows little sign of change from when it was opened in 1928. It was soon built along for much of its length, mainly with typical 1930s mock-Tudor houses. The three gleaming white 'modernist' homes make a rather startling exception.

# The Swinging '60s
# and into the '70s

Tavy Bridge, Thamesmead in 1972. The gathering is a service for a 'Week of Prayer for Christian Unity'. It is probably true to say that ecumenicalism is stronger in Thamesmead than any other part of the borough.

Welling Corner, *c.* 1963. This view which is looking east has not changed drastically in the intervening years. What has changed is the attempts at traffic management. Clearly by this date road traffic had become quite heavy at this busy junction. The absence of traffic lights must have made negotiating it rather a harrowing ordeal.

Dennis's butchers shop, Bexley High Street, 1962. At this date Dennis's shop was in the High Street, opposite Bexley Mill. Though now in Bourne Road, it is one of Bexley Village's few enduring businesses, most of which change hand with monotonous regularity.

Ethel's Stores, Blackfen Road, 1966. This picture conveys something of the 'pioneer' spirit of Blackfen. Large parts of the district, to a degree not found elsewhere in the borough, were developed in the inter-war period on a 'self build' basis, rather than as large estates. Consequently there are streets where no two houses, or bungalows, were exactly the same. Ethel's Stores offered a remarkable range of goods given its size.

Safeway, Westwood Lane, Blackfen, c. 1977. Safeway was the first 'superstore' in the borough, built in the early 1960s on the site of the Plaza Cinema (see p. 65), though now it seems small in comparison with those that have succeeded it: Sainsbury's at Crayford, Asda at Bexleyheath, Tesco at Sidcup (actually just over the borough's border with Bromley) and the latest addition, Morrison's at Erith.

Deputy Mayor Councillor Mrs M. Barron about to (ceremonially) smash the window of Hedley Mitchell's department store, Erith, 9 August 1966. This act of institutional vandalism marked the beginning of the redevelopment of Erith town centre, probably the biggest planning disaster imaginable. Streets of fine Victorian buildings were cleared to make way for a soulless concrete monstrosity. The town of Erith has never really recovered. While the recent Morrison's superstore is architecturally more appealing, it will probably depress the town centre still further.

Pier Road, Erith, 1972. Part of the new shopping centre facing mid-Victorian and Edwardian shops, which were demolished in the following year.

Erith Town Square, 1977. The new Erith shopping centre has little appeal, to say the least.

Demolition of Nelson Place, Sidcup, 1973. This small street of nineteenth-century artisans' dwellings is being demolished to make way for the Grassington Road car park. Plans for a new retail development on this site, which it is hoped will revive flagging Sidcup High Street, have been on the boil for many years.

Restoration work at Hall Place, Bexley, April 1965. In 1957 Hall Place became an annexe to the Bexley Technical High School for Girls, but by this date it was being refurbished for use as the headquarters of Bexley Libraries and Museums Department, and has subsequently housed Bexley Museum and the Bexley Local Studies Centre. The Great Hall is used for concerts and lectures. The picture shows the central staircase tower, part of the seventeenth-century section of the building. It was in such a bad state of repair that it had to be virtually rebuilt. The cost of this work was some £90,000 and the building was officially opened in May 1969.

Danson Mansion, *c*. 1973. The Ma
a grade I listed building owned by t
Council, had been empty since 197
when extensive dry rot had been
discovered and the café closed and
department offices moved elsewher
1974 the cost of restoration had r
£1 million. Conservative councillor
Archibald Forsyth was quoted as sa
'I hope the working party [to look
restoration] takes a long time and
building falls down in the meantin
Attempts to find an interested par
lease the building and restore it er
disastrously in the 1980s when th
tenant got into financial difficultie
disappeared to the Caribbean after
having removed many of the Mar
priceless fittings. Quite remarkably
the last few years the Mansion ha
partially restored thanks to a mas
injection of cash from English Her

Celebrities at the opening of the Bexleyheath Cine Bowl, April 1963. The ABC ten-pin bowling alley was demolishe
way for Asda in the 1980s. The fashionable young ladies are, from left to right, Norma Foster, Dawn Berex, Carole
the rear) and Julie Stevens.

Tony Blackburn opening Kim's Newsagents in the new Erith town centre, October 1972. Mr Blackburn was then at the height of his popularity as a Radio I disc jockey, and had also embarked on a (thankfully) short-lived singing career. As is clearly demonstrated his appeal spanned the age range.

Thamesmead, 1967. Thamesmead, unique in Greater London as a new town, was initially planned by the London County Council which identified the site on the Erith and Plumstead Marshes in the 1950s. It had the advantage that most of the site was in public ownership, and the distinct disadvantage that most of it was a low marsh with a high water table. This picture shows a general view of the site at Thamesmead, looking north east to the foundations of the tower blocks of flats in the middle distance, with early stages of linear housing in the foreground.

Thamesmead, 1970. A completed tower block can be seen on the extreme left and much of the linear housing is nearing completion. The lake (South Mere) is taking shape. In the centre is the Pyramid Social Club.

A view from one of the new tower blocks (Maplin) at Thamesmead looking towards older development at Abbey Wood, 1970. This view shows some of the maisonettes in the first phase of building which commenced in 1967. Abbey Primary School is in the mid-distance.

The Gooch family, Thamesmead's first residents who moved into their new home in Corraline Walk in July 1968. 'A great day for "pioneer family"' was the headline in the local paper when Mr and Mrs Terence Gooch and their three children were presented with an oak plaque by the leader of the Greater London Council, Desmond Plummer. Mrs Gooch was reported as saying: 'I am absolutely thrilled. It is one of the great days of my life'. The family had moved from Peckham where they lived in a pre-1914 property with no bathroom which they rented for £2 14s 6d a week. They had been on a council waiting list for nearly fourteen years. Their large maisonette at Thamesmead would cost them £4 13s a week plus rates of about £1 5s.

The North Cray Hall House, 1965. Plans for improving the North Cray Road had been in the pipeline for many years. For much of its length it was little more than a winding country lane, and carried a heavy volume of traffic. The decision was taken by Bexley Council to widen it to a four-lane dual carriageway. This work, carried out in the late 1960s, involved the destruction of much of the village of North Cray, including this row of weather-boarded cottages at right angles to the road and just across it from the White Cross pub (which fortunately survived). Local historian Peter Tester, on examining the building, found it to be an early fifteenth-century hall house. It was planned to rebuild it somewhere else in the borough, possibly at Hall Place. However, after languishing for about a decade in council storage it was given to the Weald and Downland Open Air Museum in West Sussex where it has been rebuilt.

North Cray Road, looking north, 1979. The White Cross can be seen on the left. The North Cray Hall House stood roughly opposite. In the early 1990s the local newspaper named this stretch of road 'murder mile' because of a number of fatal accidents. Local residents have campaigned for a crossing on a number of occasions, without success. Ironically this road – which was built for speed – turns into a single carriageway before it reaches Bexley. Its continuation, bypassing Bexley, has never been completed.

Erith Swimming Pool, July 1964. Erith Urban District Council was the first local authority in what is now Bexley London Borough to provide a swimming pool, in 1907. The campaign for swimming baths was spearheaded by the Erith and District Swimming Club which had been founded in the previous year. The site chosen was at the junction of Walnut Tree Road and Station Road where various other council facilities were situated on land formerly belonging to the Parish family. The open-air bath was modest, or as the local paper preferred, 'unpretentious'. In the 1950s and 1960s there was frequent lobbying for a replacement and the new Riverside Bath was opened in 1968.

The opening of Lamorbey Baths, September 1967. This scheme was initiated by the Chislehurst and Sidcup Urban District Council, which had for some years been seeking a suitable site for a covered swimming pool in the Sidcup area. The high price and shortage of land prompted them to consider the local Odeon Cinema in Halfway Street as being suitable for conversion when it became available for purchase. Though restricted in size, it was well located and the building was acquired and conversion undertaken by the council's architects. The line of the bath which measures 82 ft 6 in by 42 ft approximately follows that of the old auditorium floor, with the deep end about four feet below the original orchestra pit and basement.

The first meeting of the Council of the London Borough of Bexley, Crayford Town Hall, 1964. In the early 1960s the local government of the Greater London area was investigated, culminating in the London Local Government Act of 1963. This was not the first time that a Greater London authority had been considered and a number of services such as police and public transport already operated on a Greater London basis. The new London Boroughs were to cover larger areas and had wider powers than the authorities they replaced. Initially known as 'Borough 18', the name Bexley was chosen and elections took place in 1964. The new and old authorities met in tandem until 1965 when the London Borough of Bexley officially came into being.

The Civic Offices, Bexleyheath, under construction, *c.* 1976. Proposals for a new civic centre in Bexleyheath to centralise some of the council's disparate office accommodation and facilities were first put forward in 1967. These included a 20-storey tower block and a theatre to seat 500. By 1975 the cost of such a scheme would have been £11 million and it was abandoned in favour of a more modest scheme costing about £4 million. However, this in turn was rejected in favour of a 'value-for-money' scheme, using 'system-built' prefabricated structures. Work, which took place in four phases, began in June 1976 and was completed in January 1980. 'You pay for what you get' and the Civic Offices have no architectural merit whatsoever.

The mayoral procession arriving at Danson Park for the Town Twinning Ceremony, 25 June 1966. On this occasion Bexley 'twinned' with Evry, a suburb of Paris with some similarities to Bexley. The Mayor of Bexley, Councillor K.J. Smith and the Mayor of Evry, M. Michel Boscher, exchanged twinning oaths, coats of arms and other gifts. Behind the party is the 'boathouse' café and function rooms completed in 1964, in a rather inappropriate style for an historic park. A full programme of events to mark the occasion followed, culminating in a ball at Crayford Town Hall in the evening. A similar link was established with Nehiem Husten in Germany in 1970.

The new Queen Mary's Hospital, Sidcup, 1975. Planning for the new Queen Mary's Hospital had begun as long ago as 1959, and a phased approach was adopted, with new nurses' accommodation completed in 1965, the maternity department completed in 1966 and the accident centre and principal ward block opened in 1974. It had been built to serve Sidcup and the Cray Valley but soon after its completion it was decided that hospitals in south-east London should develop on the principle of 'co-terminosity' with their local authorities and Queen Mary's became the central acute hospital for the London Borough of Bexley despite it being only a matter of yards from the borough's southern boundary.

Southlake School, March 1974. Southlake was one of the first schools built to serve the new community of Thamesmead. Children sitting round tables in groups rather than at rows of desks had become customary by this time.

Widening the Rochester Way, *c.* 1969. This view is looking west from a newly-built footbridge. The volume of traffic had increased enormously since the 'Bexleyheath Bypass', as it was initially known, was opened in 1928. This scheme turned the road for its whole length in the borough into a six lane highway with 'improved' traffic flow at the major intersections by means of flyovers at Bourne Road and Arbuthnot Lane and an underpasses at Danson and Westwood Lane. Footbridges were introduced at other points. To the east of the borough boundary the road was rerouted further away from Dartford, causing considerable damage to Dartford Heath.

The last double-decker train on the Bexleyheath line, October 1971. This was the 6.04 p.m. (before the days of the 24-hour clock!) from Charing Cross. The double-deckers had been introduced on the line in 1949, but had not proved successful due to the problems of slow unloading. There were mixed feelings among the passengers on board. Miss Lynne Callegary of Welling said 'I like this train but nobody I tell about it believes it exists!', while William Humphreys of Erith commented 'It's a slow train, you lose time on it, and it hasn't got the speed of the other stock at all'. It was replaced by a standard ten-coach train with a seating capacity of 960 compared with the double-decker's 1,104.

'Smoky Joe', 1968. George Curnow was a well-known local character in the Bexley, Footscray, Eltham, Sidcup and Chislehurst areas from 1919 through to the 1960s. His nickname was due to the fact that he usually carried round with him (suspended from his bicycle) a bucket containing burning paper, wood or rags. He died in 1975 at the West Kent Hospital at Maidstone.

Members of BARMIE at Erith Museum, November 1979. The Bexley Association for the Refurbishment of Museum Items and Equipment were instrumental in transforming Erith Museum into the lively, entertaining and educational resource that it is today. Twenty years later and now known as the Friends of Bexley Local Museums Service (FROBLOMS), many of these people are still actively involved in voluntary work for Bexley Museums and the Local Studies and Archives Centre. Sadly, as we approach the twenty-first century, Erith Museum is under threat of closure. Erith has all too few amenities and this link with the town's rich history should be preserved.

Presentation of the Freedom of the Borou[...]
Edward Heath, MP, April 1971. Edward He[...]
who was then Prime Minister, became the [...]
person to be awarded the Freedom of the [...]
Borough of Bexley. Arguably the borough'[...]
famous political figure, he had been the M[...]
Bexley since 1950. Sir Edward Heath, as h[...]
now known, currently represents the cons[...]
of Old Bexley and Sidcup, and in the year[...]
will have chalked up fifty years of service [...]
local MP. The Freedom was conferred at a [...]
meeting of the council held at Chislehurst [...]
Sidcup Grammar School. Next to Mr Heath[...]
Mayor, Councillor Raymond Pope.

Open air service at Lesnes Abbey, 1974.
Thousands of Roman Catholics from all parts of
Bexley and Greenwich boroughs gathered at this
event to demonstrate publicly their 'love for Jesus
Christ and to renew faith'. Before the service, the
procession of the Blessed Sacrament took place
– an impressive sight of children, many dressed
in white for their First Communion, and adult
representatives of Roman Catholic churches. The
abbey ruins and the beautiful parkland in which
they are set were at this time in the care of the
Greater London Council, but since the demise of
that body in 1986 are now maintained by the
London Borough of Bexley.

A resident in the new Brampton Park Age[...]
Persons Bungalows, Bexleyheath, 1966. T[...]
scheme was built on a two-and-a-half acr[...]
between Avenue Road, Brampton Road an[...]
Blackthorn Grove, Bexleyheath and comp[...]
of thirty 'aged persons living units' in a m[...]
of flats and bungalows with a warden's h[...]
meeting room and six garages. A novel fea[...]
each unit was a high output receiver and [...]
giving direct communication with the war[...]
The cost of the scheme built by the Counc[...]
was £95,178. It was opened in April 196[...]
open fire and elderly arm chair add a degr[...]
cosiness to the scene.

# Modern Bexley

The Kelsey Brothers at Woollett Hall Farm, July 1999. It is difficult to think of any institution or business that can rival the Kelseys in terms of continuity throughout the twentieth century and indeed for much of the nineteenth century, too. The Kelseys have been farming in Bexley since about 1850, originally at Upper College Farm and since 1954 just across the river at Woollett Hall Farm in North Cray. Members of the family are recorded as having played for Bexley Cricket Club as early as 1818. David (right) and Michael Kelsey are seen outside their popular farm shop. Crops now grown on the farm include salad onions, leeks, sweetcorn, beans and kale.

Crook Log Sports Centre, Bexleyheath, under construction, 1981. The decision to build a facility offering to quality recreational opportunities for the borough's residents was made in 1979. Designed by the borough's ow Department of Architecture and Civic Design it included a main hall, measuring 36 × 32.5 × 9.2 metre high, an ancillary hall, measuring 16 × 12 metres, 6 squash courts, a conditioning gymnasium, lounge ba committee room and crèche. The building costs were £2.25 million.

Frank Bough opens the Crook Log Sports Centre, April 1982. Frank Bough was at this time one of th country's leading television sports presenters. He is seen shaking hands with Councillor Brian Samms.

Bexleyheath shopping centre under construction, 1980. A large number of premises were swept away to make way for the Broadway Centre including the much-loved Hides department store and the Lord Bexley Arms. Since this picture was taken the Astor (extreme left), Bexleyheath police station (far right), the former Bexleyheath Atheneum building (in front of the police station) and all the early Victorian shops to the left of the crane have been demolished. The result is a town centre devoid of character.

His Royal Highness the Duke of Edinburgh shares a joke with some Bexleyheath youths at the opening of the Broadway Shopping Centre in 1983. The redevelopment of Bexleyheath town centre was first mooted prior to the creation of Bexley London Borough in the 1960s. In the 1970s various schemes were considered and in the early 1980s the council produced a Bexleyheath Town Centre Plan. A public enquiry largely supported the council's proposals. Construction began in January 1980. The development by the Norwich Union Company in partnership with the borough council was completed in 1982.

An aerial view of Bexleyheath northern distributor road under construction, 1986. Considered to be a vital part of the overall redevelopment programme for Bexleyheath, work began on the northern distributor road in the spring of 1986. The road which runs from Graham Road to opposite Highland Road cost £4 million and was completed in June 1987. It was named Arnsberg Way after the district in Germany in which Bexley's twin town of Neheim Husten is situated. The picture is dominated by the rectangular block of the newly-completed Broadway Shopping Centre. The road pattern in the foreground, however, is little changed from the mid-nineteenth century.

Crayford Greyhound Stadium redevelopment, 1986. This took place in 1985 and 1986. Under an agreement
Ladbrokes and Bexley Council, the developer provided a new greyhound stadium, sports hall, supermarket, DIY s
some small industrial units. A further (supposed) community benefit was a new road, Roman Way, provided by the d
to improve the traffic flow in Crayford town centre. The new Sainsbury's and Homebase buildings dominate the l
side of the picture. The new stadium, much lacking in atmosphere compared to its predecessor, is at the top.

Inveterate library users Carol and Trevor Richardson take their daughter Emma on a trip to Sidcup Library in 1990. In 1973 the old library in Hadlow House (see p. 54) became unsafe and the library moved to temporary premises on the edge of Nelson Place car park. Hadlow House was demolished soon afterwards and the new library built on the site. It was designed by Bexley Council's Chief Architect to a brief supplied by the Chief Librarian. The 10,000 sq. ft of floor space offers considerable flexibility. The roof, however, has long been a source of leaks. It was opened by the Rt Hon Edward Heath MP in February 1981. Apart from the Central Library in Bexleyheath it remains the borough's busiest library.

Her Majesty the Queen visiting the award-winning Lakeside Health Centre, Thamesmead, 1980.

The opening of Belvedere Junior Mixed School by the Rt Hon Kenneth Baker MP, October 1987. This school in Mitchell Close was built to replace the old three-storey 'Board School' in West Street, Erith at a cost of £891,000. It has 12 classrooms and its own playing field for a capacity of 360 children. Kenneth Baker was the Education Secretary at the time. Though not universally admired by the teaching profession his name lives on in teaching circles with the system of teacher training days he instigated still being known as 'Baker days'.

Storm damage at Bedonwell School, Belvedere, October 1987. The hurricane of 16 October caused extensive structural damage to property of all types. The council immediately established emergency teams to clear debris from highways and footpaths and to make safe areas affected by fallen trees and damaged buildings. Repairs to houses, schools and public buildings were also put in hand. Trees in the borough suffered the greatest devastation and it is estimated that between 20,000 and 25,000 trees on council-owned land were lost with an additional 30,000 to 50,000 requiring surgery and removal of dangerous branches.

The A20, 1986. This picture shows the reconstruction work taking place at Crittal's Corner where a new elevated roundabout and flyover is being built to replace the old roundabout. The new section of road being constructed is seen heading off to the south of Ruxley. Rather curiously the borough boundary (between Bexley and Bromley) has not been altered to coincide with the line of the new road, but remains in the centre of the old road.

Bexleyheath Superbowl under construction, May 1988. The new ten-pin bowling alley in Oaklands Ro
opened in October 1988, replacing the original Bexleyheath Bowl in the Broadway which had been demolish
to make way for the Asda Superstore. The 28-lane, £2 million Superbowl was partly on the King George
Playing Field site and partly on the War Memorial Gardens (the burial ground of Bexleyheath's old Chapel
Ease). Needless to say this caused some controversy, particularly as it necessitated the destruction of one si
of a fine avenue of old lime trees.

Demolition of the former Regal Cinema, Bexleyheath Broadway, June 1987. The destruction of this building
make way for a new Asda superstore left Bexleyheath without any cinema whatsoever. Indeed it left only o
in the whole of the London Borough of Bexley: the ABC in Sidcup High Street.

Bexleybus no. 97 at the junction of Station Road and Sidcup High Street, *c.* 1990. The Bexleybus 'experiment' was short-lived, lasting from 1988 to 1991. It was an attempt by London Transport to counter deregulation which was creeping in elsewhere by setting up an operating arm. The cost of the tender was kept to a minimum by using very old buses, some of which were over fifteen years old, and paying staff below normal London Transport rates of pay. Bexleybus soon got an extremely bad reputation for the unreliability of its service. My abiding memory is of walking up Bourne Road on the first day of operation and seeing a Bexleybus parked with the driver carefully studying an A–Z atlas while a local schoolgirl gave him directions! In 1991 Bexleybus failed to secure the tender.

A wedding in Bexley, July 1999. The institution of marriage at the end of the twentieth century is on the decline in this country, but you would hardly believe so if you passed St Mary's Church, Bexley on a Saturday where there always seems to be a wedding taking place, and often several on the same day. Old-fashioned means of transport on these occasions are currently very popular, whether horse-drawn or otherwise. Here, newlyweds Paul and Vicky Talbott are nearly ready to be driven away in a 1928 Model A Ford.

The Swallow Hotel, Bexleyheath, late 1990s. There was some scepticism as to whether Bexleyheath could support a hotel of this size in addition to the Trusthouse Forte hotel at the Black Prince interchange on the A2. However, its proximity to the A2 and M25 and convenience for other local amenities have established its twin towers as one of Bexleyheath's notable landmarks.

Cineworld cinema complex, Bexleyheath Broadway, 1999. The last fifteen years of the twentieth century have seen an extraordinary turnaround in cinema-going in this country. So-called 'multiplex' cinemas seem to be springing up everywhere. Cineworld, opened in 1998, is a welcome addition to Bexleyheath's relatively short list of leisure amenities. Architecturally with its rather bland hints at art deco, the building lacks distinction.

The Erith–Thamesmead spine road (Bronze Age Way), looking east towards Erith, late 1990s. One would have thought that the town of Erith had suffered enough blight in the latter twentieth century, but more was to come in the 1990s with the construction of this road which had been mooted as long ago as 1976. However, every cloud has a silver lining, and during construction work some important archaeological discoveries were made, including a remarkably preserved Bronze Age trackway made out of wattle hurdles across the marshes and the foundations of a medieval manor house near St John's Church.

New housing off West Street, Erith, late 1990s. Many of the former areas of heavy industry in Erith have, in recent years, been given over to new housing. This is of course not just a local phenomenon, but indicative of the general decline in manufacturing in this country since the Second World War.

The checkout at Morrison's superstore, Erith, July 1999. Patterns of shopping have changed incredibly during the course of the century. Most shopping is now done in huge stores such as this, generally in 'out of town' sites necessitating a car journey. It is now possible to shop on Sundays and, on weekdays, for 24 hours in the day. It is hoped that this store, which opened in 1998, will play a part in the regeneration of Erith. But this remains to be seen.

Woolwich Building Society Headquarters, Bexleyheath, late 1990s. The Woolwich is one of the largest employers in the borough. This appealing building, completed in the 1980s, is a landmark which can be seen from quite a distance. The Royal Albert pub is fast becoming the oldest building in this part of Bexleyheath.

The Acorn Retail Estate, Crayford, July 1999. This picture, taken on a Sunday morning, shows this recently-opened retail park built on the site of the former Vickers works. Late twentieth-century Britain is a place for buying and selling and not for making. Crayfordians had many reservations about this development, not least about the increased traffic that would be generated. One good thing, though, has been the restoration of the clocktower (in front of McDonald's drive-in restaurant) built in 1902 and in a derelict state for many years. It is also pleasing to note, on the left, the survival of Crayford Town Hall, built by Vickers as a canteen for their workers in 1915, which the Conservative-controlled council was to have demolished in the early 1990s, but which the subsequent Labour/Liberal Democrat 'coalition' reprieved.

Bar Lorca, Bexley High Street, July 1999. Bexley High Street has a growing number of popular eating and drinking places. This tapas bar is the latest addition, recently having been converted from a bank. Many local branches of banks and building societies have closed in recent years.

The King's Head, Bexley, 1999.
People have sat outside this
pub enjoying a pint of ale,
for centuries. Long may it
continue!

A Millennium Pageant at Old Bexley Church of England School, July 1999. As the century draws to a close, millennium fever is gripping the nation, and Old Bexley C of E School struck early by holding a celebratory event in the summer of 1999. Every child in the school took part and put on a splendid display of events from the history of the last 1,000 years. Here we see the whole cast gathered for the finale.

Two members of the cast from Old Bexley C of E School's Millennium Pageant: Lucy (left), a 1950s rock & roll dancer, and Maddy Barr-Hamilton, a fifteenth-century courtier with headteacher Mr C.J. Roberts (an eighteenth-century officer), July 1999.

# Acknowledgements and Picture Credits

Thanks are due to Stuart Bligh, Local Studies Manager, and the staff – Oliver Wooller, Frances Sweeny and Sue Barclay – of the Bexley Local Studies and Archives Centre for their patient assistance and constant supply of coffee; most of the pictures are from the collections of the Bexley Local Studies Centre but many thanks are due to Ken Chamberlain, David Gillham, Martyn Nicholls, Iris Brooker, Iris Burton and Sybil Burton for access to their collections of photographs; to Colourwise Photography in Crayford, and Robert Anthony Photographics in Bethnal Green; to the Topham Picture Source, Bexley Cricket Club and Keith Turnbull for permission to use photographs; to Ann Brunton, Roger Hill, David and Michael Kelsey, Jim Packer, Freda Skinner, Ted Thomas and Joan Wallace for information and help; but chiefly to my wife, Tanya Sangster, who pampered me very effectively while this book was being written.

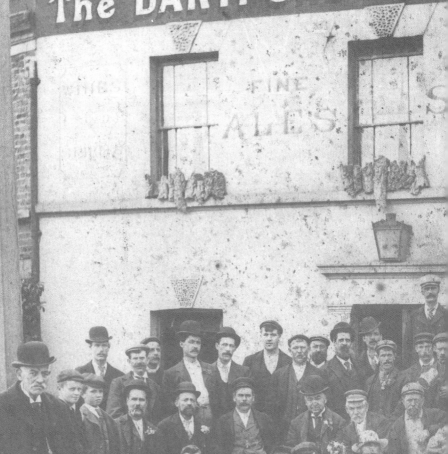